ATTITUDE IS EVERYTHING: SURVIVING CANCER COLORING FOR WELLNESS JOURNAL

An Interactive Coloring Journal

For Warriors Battling Cancer

MARENDA TAYLOR

ISBN-13. 978-1540612366

Printed in the United States of America

Inspiration, Meditation, and Relaxation!

A cancer diagnosis at any stage of life is devastating. There will be good days and bad days. The most important thing to remember is **ATTITUDE is EVERYTHING**. This interactive coloring for wellness journal will help you maintain the mindset of a champion and a winning attitude.

This book created by a cancer survivor for cancer survivors, combines coloring and writing for wellness using basic to intricate meditative designs with inspirational messages, journal entry pages, and affirmations to help you creatively express yourself, cope with chemo brain, tame monkey mind, reduce stress, lower anxiety, decrease negative emotions, and maintain a positive attitude while inspiring you to live every day of your life abundantly.

There are 3 specific types of pages:

- Journal Entry
- Coloring
- Affirmation

The journal entry pages have an inspirational message to help guide your thoughts for writing and include a design for coloring. It is suggested that you use colored pencils for coloring the designs and an ink or gel pen for writing.

The full coloring pages are best colored with coloring pencils. Markers may bleed through the page.

The affirmation pages have affirmations that are best read out loud 3 or more times. It is highly recommended that the affirmations be repeated often.

There are no rules about how you use this book or what order you complete the pages. The only advice is that you approach each page with an open heart and an open mind.

Start coloring, writing, and healing!

"You can be a victim of cancer, or a survivor of cancer. It's a mindset."
~Dave Pelzer

Date:_____

_____

_____

_____

_____

_____

_____

_____

_____

_____

_____

AFFIRMATIONS

Hope is realistic.

My thoughts shape my reality.

When I am open to seeing miracles,
I am more likely to notice them.

My happiness and gratitude grow.

Today, I choose to be hopeful.

I focus on the positive aspects of my life.

"An affirmation is a strong positive statement that somthing is already so." ~Shakti Gawain

Date:_____

_____

_____

_____

_____

_____

_____

_____

_____

_____

_____

AFFIRMATIONS

Instead of resisting what is in front of me, I take hold of it. I use it to my advantage and come out successfully at the end. This approach allows me to accept my situation.

Today, my focus is on making the most of whatever life lays before me. I accept that the experiences of today are the ones I am meant to have. I am content with where I am today because I know it prepares me for better things tomorrow.

"Absorb what is useful. Discard what is not.
Add what is uniquely your own."
~Bruce Lee

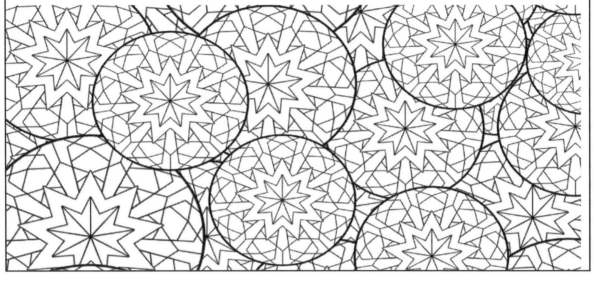

Date:_____

AFFIRMATIONS

When I wake up each day, I focus on my blessings. I think about how fortunate I am to have them. My gratitude carries through the entire day and keeps me at peace.

Today, I am committed to having only happy moments. Even when negative circumstances come my way, I spin them and find the positive. My life is a testament to how to make the best out of any situation. I am an optimistic life force.

"Words are also actions, and actions are a kind of words."
Ralph Waldo Emerson

Date:_____

_____

_____

_____

_____

_____

_____

_____

_____

_____

_____

AFFIRMATIONS

I engage fully with each of my physical senses to experience more joy.

I enjoy hugs from friends and the touch of the sun warming my skin. I listen to birds singing and rain pouring down. I savor the fragrance of rose gardens and soup simmering on the stove.

Today, I thank my body for showing me how to take care of my mental and physical well being. I treat my body like a good friend and wise teacher.

"Adversity causes some men to break; others to break records"
~William Ward

Date:_____

_____

_____

_____

_____

_____

_____

_____

_____

_____

_____

AFFIRMATIONS

My life has challenges, but I overcome them and still find success and joy.

I focus on the positive aspects of my life and know my dreams are in the process of coming true, regardless of my current situation.

I know that adversity is just a temporary block. When I come across obstacles in my path, I hardly stumble. I immediately look for a way to get around them. I find myself getting stronger and stronger as I successfully conquer each hardship and continue to move forward

"Change the changeable accept the unchangeable and remove yourself from the unacceptable." **~Denis Waitley**

Date:_____

_____

_____

_____

_____

_____

_____

_____

_____

_____

_____

_____

AFFIRMATIONS

I curiously and bravely face the unknown.

When life throws me a curve ball, I stand tall and handle the uncertainty that comes with it. I exercise unbridled bravery about the future.

My doubt is easily replaced by curiosity when I am faced with an unfamiliar situation. I look at newness as a chance to learn more about myself. New situations expose me to the extent of my skill sets.

**"Be courageous. Otherwise you will never experience what life has to offer."
~Unknown**

Date:_____

_____

_____

_____

_____

_____

_____

_____

_____

_____

_____

AFFIRMATIONS

Today, the uncertainties of life are more of a challenge to me than a concern. I look at them as opportunities to find answers.

I am committed to being brave during unfamiliar situations and finding the positive experience in them.

"Concentrated thoughts produce desired results."
~Zig Ziglar

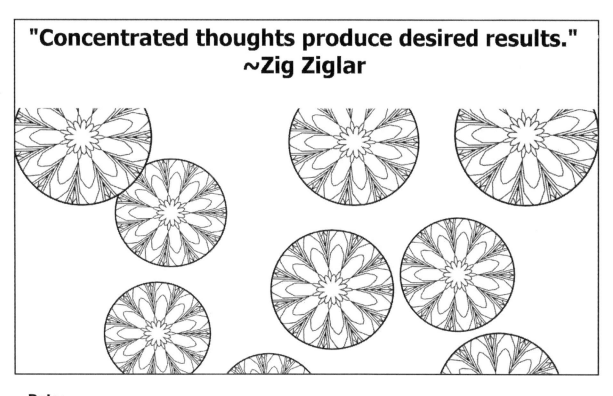

Date:_____

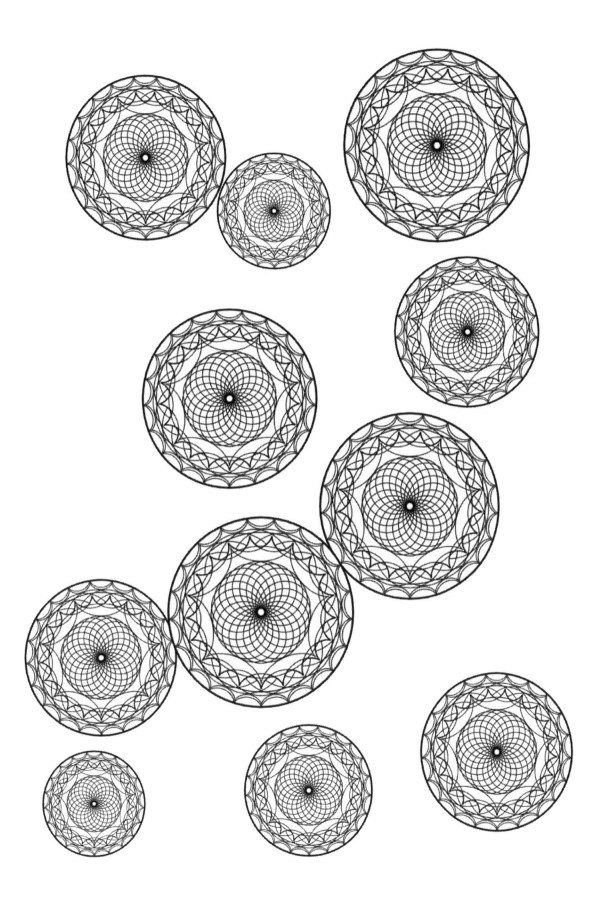

AFFIRMATIONS

Today, I sit down to meditate. I explore my thoughts and learn to appreciate myself.

Meditation gives me an opportunity to discover my true self. Observing my thoughts prepares me to live the life I really want.

I tune out distractions. My concentration grows stronger. I pay attention to how my mind works. I listen to my inner voice.

"Words have energy and power with the ability to help,
to heal, to hinder, to hurt, to harm,
to humiliate, and to humble." -Yehuda Berg

Date:_____

_____

_____

_____

_____

_____

_____

_____

_____

_____

AFFIRMATIONS

Today, my peace of mind comes from living an authentic life. I commit to remaining true to myself and being honest with others. Each day is a chance to renew that commitment.

I live an authentic life.

I live my life according to my own principles. The outside world has very little impact on my choices. I am proud to be true to myself and have a strong sense of purpose.

"Everytime you smile at someone it is an action of love a gift to that person a beautiful thing." ~Mother Teresa

Date:_____

_____

_____

_____

_____

_____

_____

_____

_____

_____

_____

_____

AFFIRMATIONS

Today, my peace of mind comes from living an authentic life. I commit to remaining true to myself and being honest with others. Each day is a chance to renew that commitment.

I live an authentic life.

I live my life according to my own principles. The outside world has very little impact on my choices. I am proud to be true to myself and have a strong sense of purpose.

"Always remember that the future comes one day at a time." ~Dean Acheson

Date:_____

_____

_____

_____

_____

_____

_____

_____

_____

_____

_____

AFFIRMATIONS

I thank others for their kindness. I remember the good things that they contribute to my life.

I admire the good qualities of others.

To generate loving thoughts, I start with my family and friends. I recall my warm feelings towards them. I imagine bringing that emotion into my communications with the rest of the world.

If I become tense or irritated, I use my breath to restore my loving thoughts. I cherish myself as I breathe in. I cherish others as I breathe out.

**"We must embrace pain
and burn it as fuel for our journey."
~Kenji Miyazawa**

Date:_____

_____

_____

_____

_____

_____

_____

_____

_____

_____

_____

AFFIRMATIONS

This moment is precious to me.

I treasure each moment. I am committed to living in the present.

I put aside past disappointments and expectations for the future. I focus on what is happening right now. I give my full attention to whatever I am doing.

I train myself to breathe fully and deeply. I slow down. I notice the air entering and exiting my nostrils. I fill my abdomen and chest with each inhalation and let them sink with each gentle exhalation. I create a soothing rhythm.

"Toughness is in the soul and spirit, not in muscles." ~Alex Karras

Date:_____

_____

_____

_____

_____

_____

_____

_____

_____

_____

_____

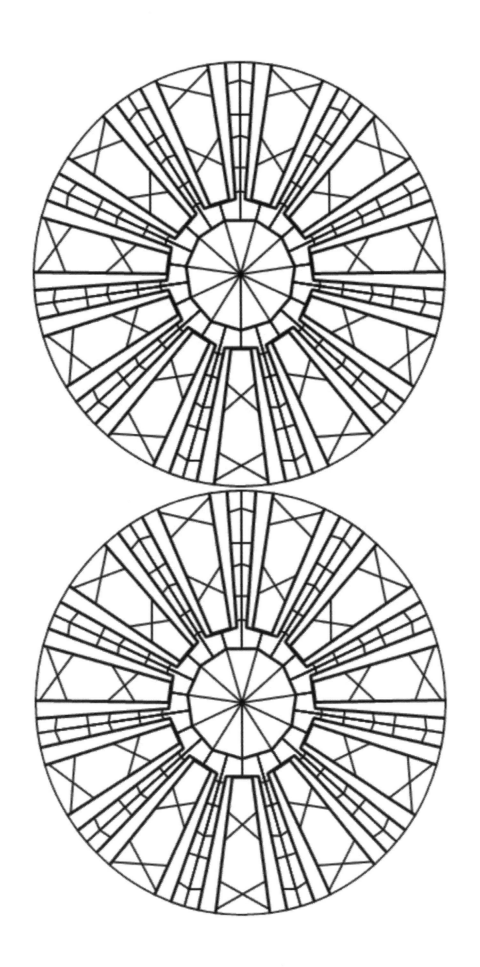

AFFIRMATIONS

Life is often turbulent. I remain steadfast in my commitments and resilient during the most challenging moments. The hurricane of transformation alters the landscape. I remain unmoved by the strongest gusts. I am firm.

Whatever the winds of adversity throw at me, I persevere.

I weather the longest storms. With each passing gale, the earth around me wears away. Somehow I stand taller, my presence is greater. I am a rock, and then a boulder. Soon, I am a mountain.

"A strong person and a waterfall always channel their own path."
~Unknown

Date:_____

_____

_____

_____

_____

_____

_____

_____

_____

_____

_____

AFFIRMATIONS

I realize that stress or contentment comes from my thoughts rather than from external forces. I am at peace as long as I accept what each moment brings. Sometimes I am comfortable and sometimes I learn and grow by overcoming challenges.

Today, I free myself from old habits and assumptions that could hold me back. I appreciate each moment for what it is.

"Begin at once to live and count each separate day as a separate life."
~Seneca

Date:_____

_____

_____

_____

_____

_____

_____

_____

_____

_____

_____

AFFIRMATIONS

My life is more enjoyable when I have **reasons** to be happy, and passion for whatever I am involved in provides me with all the reasons I could ever desire.

Today, I look forward to new experiences. I want to engage in all the wonderment that each day can bring.

"Words are seeds that do more than blow around.
They land in our hearts and not the ground.
Be careful what you plant and careful what you say.
You might have to eat what you planted one day." -Unknown

Date:_____

_____

_____

_____

_____

_____

_____

_____

_____

_____

_____

_____

AFFIRMATIONS

I trust in the process of life.

Life is a wonderful mystery, and I am content to let it unfold. While others might complain and struggle, I can see that life has its own process. I trust that process even if I lack complete understanding.

Life is a miraculous thing. All the answers come in time. While the reasons may be a mystery to me, I know that there is a purpose to everything in my life.

> **"Concentration is the ability to think about absolutely nothing when it is absolutely necessary."**
> **~Ray Knight**

Date:_____

_____

_____

_____

_____

_____

_____

_____

_____

_____

_____

AFFIRMATIONS

Taking care of my soul is another way to replenish my life. I use self-reflection and prayer to make sure I stay true to my passions, purpose, and relationships. Nurturing my soul is a valuable part of my daily routine.

I am grateful for the gifts of my mind, body, and soul, so I do my best to replenish them. Finding time to take care of myself is vital. Loving and nurturing my mind, body, and soul bring me health, happiness and fulfillment.

"Faith is to believe what you do not see; the reward of this faith is to see what you believe."
~Saint Augustine

Date:_____

_____

_____

_____

_____

_____

_____

_____

_____

_____

_____

AFFIRMATIONS

Taking care of my soul is another way to replenish my life. I use self-reflection and prayer to make sure I stay true to my passions, purpose, and relationships.

Nurturing my soul is a valuable part of my daily routine.

I am grateful for the gifts of my mind, body, and soul, so I do my best to replenish them. Finding time to take care of myself is vital. Loving and nurturing my mind, body, and soul bring me health, happiness and fulfillment.

**"A grateful mind is a great mind
that eventually attracts to it great things"
~Plato**

Date:_____

_____

_____

_____

_____

_____

_____

_____

_____

_____

_____

AFFIRMATIONS

I regularly attract the things that are for my highest good. Sometimes those things are enjoyable and sometimes they are less than pleasant. But they are all in my best interest. I appreciate everything that comes into my life.

I am a magnet that attracts what is good for me. As a result, I am wise and my mind guides me in a positive direction, regardless of the circumstance. I embrace situations that help me learn, grow, and thrive. I love this about myself.

Today, I realize that whatever I attract is helpful for me in some way. I am grateful that the universe is providing me with the tools to excel in life.

.

"Miracles come in moments.
Be ready and willing." ~Wayne Dyer

Date:_____

_____

_____

_____

_____

_____

_____

_____

_____

_____

_____

AFFIRMATIONS

My outlook on life is infused with enthusiasm.

I have a wonderful outlook on life. Each day, I am blessed to live a life filled with joyful anticipation. This expectation for good things is the source of my great enthusiasm.

I plan exciting things into my schedule on a regular basis. My life is exciting and fulfilling.

I have a great life and I expect even greater things in the future. Full speed ahead! I feel unstoppable as I welcome the good things to come.

When I feel less than enthusiastic about my life, I examine my feelings and find the source. I can then quickly make any necessary changes and my enthusiasm is restored. I find the process to be simple and easy.

"Do not waste time calculating your chances of success and failure. Just fix your aim and begin." ~Guan Yin Tzu

Date:_____

_____

_____

_____

_____

_____

_____

_____

_____

_____

_____

_____

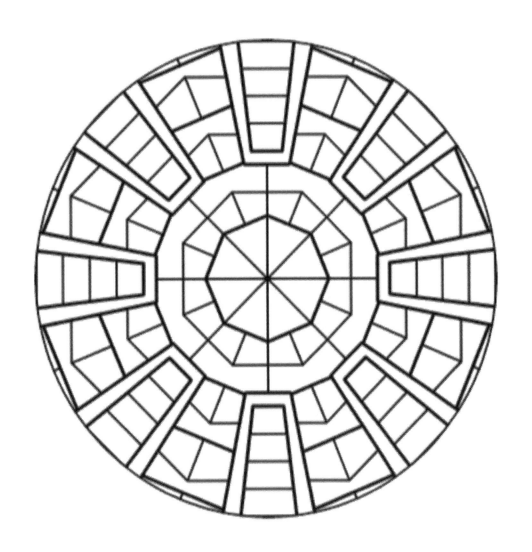

AFFIRMATIONS

My dreams are one of my top priorities.

While I have many responsibilities, my dreams are always a top priority. I realize that dreams are what make life worth living.

I regularly schedule time to work on my dreams. Each day, I spend at least an hour towards making my dreams become a reality.

My dreams are worthy of my time.

It can be easy to become sidetracked, but I always remember to focus on my dreams.

Today, my dreams are one of my top priorities. I realize that everything else exists to support my dreams. Making my dreams come true is up to me and I am up to the challenge.

> **"Human beings, by changing the inner attitudes of their minds, can change the outer aspects of their lives."**
> **~William James**

Date:_____

_____

_____

_____

_____

_____

_____

_____

_____

_____

_____

AFFIRMATIONS

I value the ability to change and I do everything I can to improve my life and myself. I remind myself each day that I am capable of changing any part of my life at any moment.

I realize that the key to change is belief. I believe in myself. I believe that the past can be quite different than the future. Therefore, change is possible for me.

As I make positive changes, I find my life gets easier every day. Change can bring great things into my life and I now look forward to making changes.

Today, I renew my commitment to changing and improving myself. I know I can change quickly and easily. I am a strong person. I have the power to change myself.

"Life is without meaning. You bring the meaning to it. The meaning of life is whatever you ascribe it to be. Being alive is the meaning." ~Joseph Campbell

Date:_____

_____

_____

_____

_____

_____

_____

_____

_____

_____

_____

AFFIRMATIONS

What I do makes a difference.

Even the little things matter. Everything I do makes a difference.

My actions set an example for others.

Each time I take a step forward, it brings me closer to my goals.

Recognizing my impact frees me from apathy and discouragement. I am motivated to put forth my best efforts.

Today, I feel joyful and confident. I know that everything I do contributes to making the world a better place.

"To fear is one thing. To let fear grab you by the tail and swing you around is another."
~Katherine Paterson

Date:_____

_____

_____

_____

_____

_____

_____

_____

_____

_____

_____

AFFIRMATIONS

What I do makes a difference.

Even the little things matter. Everything I do makes a difference.

My actions set an example for others.

Each time I take a step forward, it brings me closer to my goals.

Recognizing my impact frees me from apathy and discouragement. I am motivated to put forth my best efforts.

Today, I feel joyful and confident. I know that everything I do contributes to making the world a better place.

"It is sometimes too difficult to put into words."
~Unknown

Date:_____

_____

_____

_____

_____

_____

_____

_____

_____

_____

AFFIRMATIONS

Fear is no match for my strong spirit and will.

My will and my spirit are stronger than any dart of fear aimed in my direction. When disappointment strikes, I remain confident in myself because I am certain that great success is within my reach.

Though fear may relentlessly try to come against me, my strong will helps me reject fear over and over again. I carry on in my journey with a positive attitude because my spirit is too strong to be broken. I dance through the streets of my destiny to the melody of joy, thanks to the invincible spirit within me.

I can accomplish anything I set my mind to when I am determined.

"Scars are tattoos with better stories."
~ Unknown

Date:_____

_____

_____

_____

_____

_____

_____

_____

_____

_____

_____

_____

AFFIRMATIONS

Today, I look in the mirror and see a divine creation. I commit to loving the person who looks back at me because I am truly blessed.

"Going in one more round when you don't think you can – that's what makes all the difference in your life."
~Rocky

Date:_____

_____

_____

_____

_____

_____

_____

_____

_____

_____

AFFIRMATIONS

Happiness is simplicity.

I love that my life is free of complexities. My inner peace comes from living a simple life.

I find happiness in simplicity. My senses are heightened when I participate in life's simple pleasures. I refrain from worrying about unmanageable situations.

Today, I enjoy a simple lifestyle. I rest well at night when I avoid complex, daunting situations. And with adequate rest, I have the energy to take on a new day. My mission is to make every day fulfilling and worthwhile. I aim to do that by keeping things simple.

For More Books:

MarendaTaylor.com

Manufactured by Amazon.ca
Bolton, ON

16381695R00094